Ancient MAYA CULTURE

Christine Honders

PowerKids press

NEW YORK

Published in 2017 by The Rosen Publishing Group, Inc.
29 East 21st Street, New York, NY 10010

Editor: Caitlin McAneney
Book Design: Mickey Harmon

Photo Credits: Cover piotreknik/Shutterstock.com; p. 5 DC_Aperture/Shutterstock.com; pp. 6, 9 SarkaSch/
Shutterstock.com; p. 7 SarkaSch/Shutterstock.com; p. 8 jejim/Shutterstock.com; p. 11 Svetlana Bykova/
Shutterstock.com; p. 13 f9photos/Shutterstock.com; p. 14 Fer Gregory/Shutterstock.com; p. 15 Werner Forman/
Contributor/Universal Images Group/Getty Images; p. 17 Heritage Images/Hulton Fine Art Collection/Getty
Images; p. 18 https://en.wikipedia.org/wiki/Popol_Vuh#/media/File:Popol_vuh.jpg; p. 19 https://commons.
wikimedia.org/wiki/File:Hero_Twins.JPG; p. 21 Leon Rafael/Shutterstock.com; p. 22 https://upload.wikimedia.
org/wikipedia/commons/1/10/CodexPages6_8.jpg; p. 25 https://commons.wikimedia.org/wiki/File:Takalik_Abaj_
Stela_5_p4.jpg; p. 26 DEA/C. SAPPA/Contributor/De Agostini/Getty Images; p. 27 KKulikov/Shutterstock.com;
p. 28 DEA/C. SAPPA/De Agostini/Getty Images; p. 29 https://upload.wikimedia.org/wikipedia/commons/c/c2/
Mexican_maya_codex.jpg.

Library of Congress Cataloging-in-Publication Data

Names: Honders, Christine, author.
Title: Ancient Maya culture / Christine Honders.
Description: New York : PowerKids Press, 2017. | Series: Spotlight on the
   Maya, Aztec, and Inca civilizations | Includes index.
Identifiers: LCCN 2016002138 | ISBN 9781499419580 (pbk.) | ISBN 9781499419610 (library bound) | ISBN
9781499419597 (6 pack)
Subjects: LCSH: Mayas--History--Juvenile literature. | Mayas--Social life and
   customs--Juvenile literature.
Classification: LCC F1435 .H765 2017 | DDC 972.81--dc23
LC record available at http://lccn.loc.gov/2016002138

CPSIA Compliance Information: Batch #BS16PK: For further information contact Rosen Publishing, New York, New York at 1-800-237-9932.

CONTENTS

WHO WERE THE ANCIENT MAYA?

The Maya civilization had one of the most advanced cultures in Mesoamerica, which includes part of today's Mexico and Central America. While other **indigenous** people were scattered all over Mesoamerica, the Maya were centered on the Yucatán Peninsula and part of Central America. This helped protect them from invasion by other Mesoamerican groups and allowed them to rule the region for many years.

The Maya Empire reached its peak around AD 500. By this time, the Maya had established a very strong culture. Culture is the beliefs, values, knowledge, and customs of a group of people. The ancient Maya had many gods, and religion was the center of their culture. It's easy to see how important religion was when studying Maya architecture, pyramids, astronomy, mathematics, and even sporting events. Maya beliefs also inspired them to become one of the first ancient civilizations to develop a calendar.

When some Maya ruins were first discovered, European explorers thought the cities were too well built to be constructed by the Maya. They assumed the ruins were left by other great civilizations, such as the Romans or Egyptians.

EARLY INFLUENCES

The history of Mesoamerica is divided into periods. The first Maya settlements existed around 1800 BC in the Pre-Classic Period. During this time, the Maya became skilled farmers, inventing new **techniques** to grow their crops. A nearby Mesoamerican civilization, the Olmecs, flourished during the Pre-Classic Period. They were the first in the area to build great cities and monuments with stone and brick,

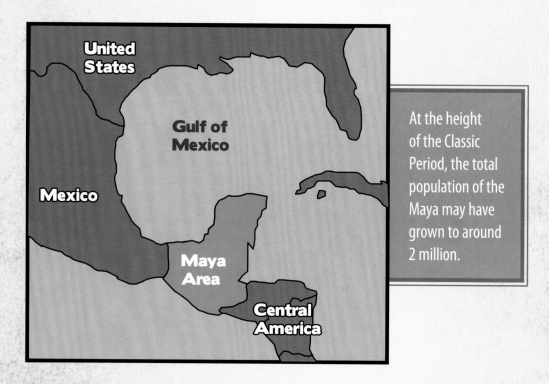

United States

Gulf of Mexico

Mexico

Maya Area

Central America

At the height of the Classic Period, the total population of the Maya may have grown to around 2 million.

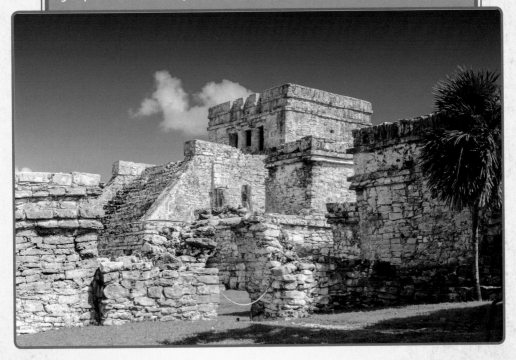

Maya ruins still stand across the Yucatán Peninsula today. They give us a glimpse into ancient Maya culture.

and they were talented sculptors. The Maya got many of their cultural traits from the Olmec people.

The Maya culture reached its height during the Classic Period, which lasted from AD 250 to AD 900. During this time, nearly 40 Maya cities existed around the lowland forests throughout their region. This time period is the most famous in Maya history and is known as the golden age of Maya civilization. This book will highlight the advancements of Maya culture during the Classic Period.

MAYA ARCHITECTURE

The Maya were famous for their architecture and highly decorated stone cities. Maya cities were known as city-states. Each city-state had one large city that ruled over the surrounding area. Each had its own king, who lived in a large palace with his family. The Maya also built pyramids

Before the discovery of King Pakal's tomb in the Temple of the Inscriptions, people thought the Maya built pyramids just as temples for their gods. Pakal's tomb was the first Maya royal tomb ever to be excavated, or uncovered.

These are Maya ruins of the ancient city of Tulum, which is on the Caribbean coast in today's Mexican state of Quintana Roo.

and public buildings that were covered with carvings and statues in honor of their gods and their kings.

One of the most famous palaces is found in the city of Palenque. King Pakal the Great enlarged the palace during his rule. The palace included many rooms, courts for public events, and a four-story tower. Palenque is also home to the Temple of the Inscriptions, a famous stepped pyramid with nine levels. In 1952, a Mexican **archaeologist** discovered a stairway hidden below the floor of the temple. It led to a tomb where King Pakal was buried!

CULTURE IN TIKAL

Tikal was one of the largest and most powerful Maya city-states, located in what is now known as Guatemala. In 378 AD, forces from a powerful nearby city arrived at Tikal. Some historians suggest it was a violent takeover, since Tikal's original ruler died the same day. Eventually, the invaders' culture influenced Tikal clothing, art, and architecture.

The height of Tikal was from around AD 600 to 900. The city spread over 50 square miles (129.5 sq km) with a population of more than 60,000 people. It had over 3,000 structures, including 24 pyramids. The twin pyramid complexes were some of Tikal's most massive building projects. Starting by AD 672, twin pyramids were built facing each other at the end of each *k'atun*. A *k'atun* is a 20-year period in the Maya calendar. Nine of these twin pyramid complexes have been found in Tikal.

The North Acropolis in Tikal contained the tombs of the city's early kings. One of the most decorated tombs was for King Yax Nuun Ayiin, nicknamed "Curl Nose." He was buried in fine clothing with nine **sacrificial** victims. He was surrounded by pots of cacao (used to make chocolate) and maize.

PYRAMIDS

Maya pyramids tell us a lot about their culture. They have a special stepped shape, which represents the *witz*. *Witz* means "mountain," especially the holy mountain of the gods. The ancient Maya believed their gods lived on top of mountains, which were symbols of power and centers of spiritual energy for all living things. The Maya built pyramids in every city-state to make the **patron** god of that city feel at home.

The Maya built two kinds of pyramids. The first had a temple on the top, which was used as a place for priests to perform religious ceremonies. The second kind was a sacred pyramid built to honor a god. These pyramids had steeper steps and weren't meant to be touched by humans. Maya pyramids were often built over older pyramids. This was to honor the current ruler and to renew his relationship with the gods.

This is the Pyramid of the Magician in the city of Uxmal in today's Mexico. According to Maya legend, it was built by the god Itzamna in one night and was used as a school to train healers and priests.

The Maya were very precise, or exact, in planning their cities. They built pyramids based on their understanding of the gods because religion was central to their culture. They made sure the pyramids faced in certain directions, and often angled them so they'd face sunrise or sunset depending on the time of year.

El Castillo, the main pyramid in the city of Chichén Itzá, was built for the god Kukulkan ("feathered serpent"). Each of the four sides of the pyramid has 91 steps, and when

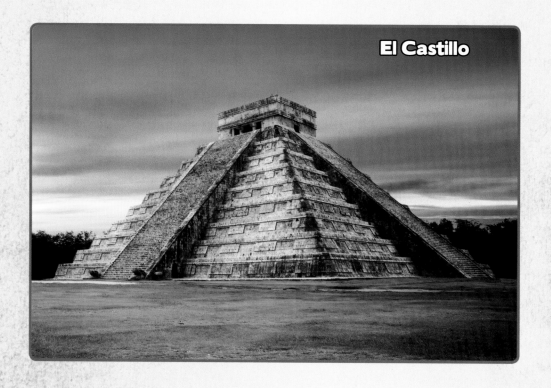

El Castillo

added to the top platform step, this equals 365 steps, one for each day of the Maya year. Two stone serpent heads are at the base of one set of stairs. During the spring and autumn **equinoxes**, the shadow caused by the setting sun looks like a serpent moving down the stairs, representing the god's return to Earth twice a year to give his blessings.

Kukulkan was one of the most important gods of the Maya. He was shown as a feathered snake. He helped create the world and taught the people about civilization.

MAYA RELIGION

The Maya belief in their **pantheon** greatly affected their culture. They believed their gods were a major part of their daily lives and that all things contained an unseen power called *k'uh*, which means "sacredness." They believed the universe was divided into three parts: Earth, sky, and Xibalba, or the underworld. Xibalba was terrifying to the Maya. In fact, they thought if they didn't worship correctly, the demons from the underworld would come to Earth and attack them.

The ancient Maya believed the afterlife was a journey towards paradise, but it was a frightening one. Everyone started by attempting to cross the underworld, where gods with names like Bloody Teeth or Flying Scab would scare people and point them in the wrong direction. Then, there were nine levels to climb before reaching Earth, and 13 more levels until they finally reached heaven.

This is the lid of King Pakal's **sarcophagus** showing Pakal falling into Xibalba.

The only existing Maya religious text is called the Popol Vuh, also known as *The Light That Came from Beside the Sea.* The Popol Vuh tells the stories of how Earth and human beings were created, and it describes the beliefs of the Maya. A large part of Maya religious beliefs involved the stars and planets. They scheduled their ceremonies and rituals based

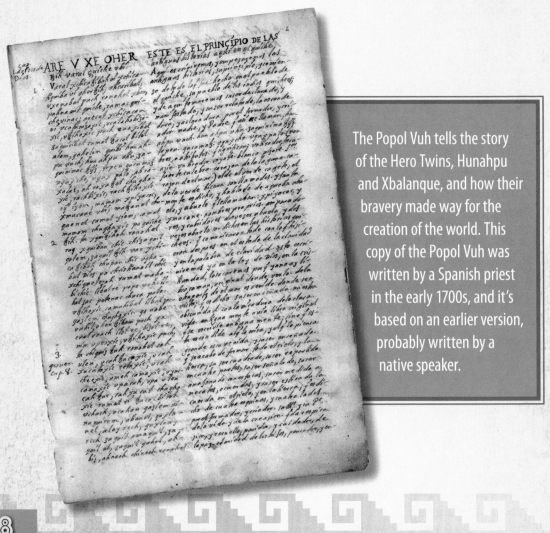

The Popol Vuh tells the story of the Hero Twins, Hunahpu and Xbalanque, and how their bravery made way for the creation of the world. This copy of the Popol Vuh was written by a Spanish priest in the early 1700s, and it's based on an earlier version, probably written by a native speaker.

This artwork shows the Maya Hero Twins, who are the main heroes of the Popol Vuh.

on where the stars were positioned on a particular day. They believed the **cyclical** pattern of the stars and planets represented life.

The ancient Maya practiced human sacrifice as part of their religion. To the Maya, nothing was ever really born and nothing ever really died, so the person sacrificed simply "moved on" to their journey into the afterlife. Humans were sacrificed as gifts to the gods. In return, the person sacrificed didn't have to travel through the underworld and instead went straight to heaven.

THE GODS OF THE MAYA

The ancient Maya believed in over 250 gods and thought they affected every part of their daily lives. The god of the woods, Yum Caax, protected the rain forests, crops, and animals. Chaac was the god of rain and lightning. When he was happy, he would use his lightning axe to strike the clouds and make the rain fall. The gods controlled the weather, the harvest, how people dressed, and even who they married. Each city had its own god who was invited to live in the central temple. Upon accepting the invitation, the god made sure the city would prosper.

One of the most important gods of the pantheon was Itzamna, the god of fire. The Maya believed he ruled heaven and controlled day and night. They also believed he created their calendar and taught them their systems of writing, mathematics, and agriculture.

The Maya kings were treated almost as gods themselves. They performed rituals where they fasted, smoked tobacco, and spilled their own blood so they'd have "visions" to be able to communicate with the gods.

MASTERS OF MATHEMATICS AND WRITING

The Maya had one of the most advanced systems of writing of all the civilizations in Mesoamerica. They used a form of writing called hieroglyphics. Symbols, called glyphs, represented different objects, words, or sounds, and they were put together to form sentences and tell stories. The only people who learned to read and write were priests and nobles. They wrote on long pieces of paper made of bark or leather that folded up to make books. Maya books are called codices.

The Dresden Codex is a book of Maya writings. It's considered the best preserved and oldest of all surviving Maya manuscripts.

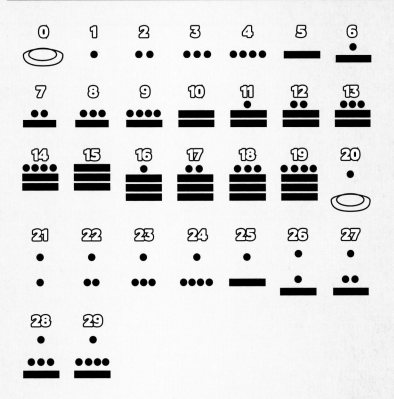

The Maya were also one of the first civilizations to come up with a number system that used the concept of zero, which was drawn to look like a shell. The system was also made up of a series of dots and bars. Each dot represented one item, and each bar represented five items. After every four dots, another bar would be added. A dot over a shell represented 20.

THE MAYA CALENDAR

Just like everything else in their culture, the invention of the Maya calendar was driven by their religious beliefs. Priests and **scribes** studied mathematics and astronomy so they could understand the stars and planets and what the gods meant to tell them by their positions in the sky. This led to the creation of the sacred calendar.

The Maya had three calendars. The sacred calendar, Tzolk'in, was used to predict the future and chart the stars. It was made up of 260 days with two cycles, a 20-day cycle, and 13-day cycle. Haab', the solar calendar, marked the days and seasons. It had 18 months of 20 days each with five extra days, making 365 days in the year. The third calendar, the Long Count, was used to record history. It started on what we would call August 11, 3114 BC—the day the Maya believed Earth was created.

This carved stone found in Guatemala shows an early example of a Long Count date.

POK-A-TOK

The Maya ball game, called Pok-a-Tok, meant a great deal to Maya culture. It was a sacred game that represented the human struggle between life and death. There were two teams of seven players in each game. The court had sloping walls and small stone hoops attached high on the walls. The object was for the players to get a small rubber ball through the hoops without touching it with their hands or feet. The game was so difficult that it could go on for days, and so rough people often died playing it.

There was usually a sacrifice at the end of the game. Some historians think the losing team was killed, but others believe the Maya would never give a losing team as a gift to their gods. These historians believe the Maya beheaded the winning captain or even the whole team, who were then sent directly to heaven.

This is a Maya ball court where games of Pok-a-Tok would be played. The religious importance of Pok-a-Tok was described in the Popol Vuh with a story of two brothers who were excellent players. One brother would go on to father the legendary Hero Twins, who were also very talented ball players.

THE MYSTERIOUS END

Between the late 700s and 900, something happened that caused the decline of Maya civilization. Historians have different theories explaining why, but no one knows for sure. One theory is that the large populations of the city-states overused the surrounding land, which led to deforestation, or the destruction of forests. Without natural resources, it was impossible to keep these cities thriving. Others believe constant war between the cities caused the relationships between them to break down. A third theory is that a major environmental change, most likely a **drought**, wiped out the Maya's food and water supplies.

The Spanish founded the city of Mérida within the Maya region in 1542. This Spanish coat of arms was carved into a cathedral in Mérida after its founding.

The Spanish invasion changed the Maya world forever. They forced the Maya to accept Christianity as their religion and burned nearly all their books. Only four codices are left in existence.

Not every city-state was abandoned at the same time. Chichén Itzá continued to grow and prosper from about 900 to 1200. When Spanish invaders came in the 1500s, most of the Maya were living in small farming villages. Their great cities had become overgrown and taken over by the jungles of Mesoamerica.

MAYA CULTURE TODAY

Although the great cities of the Maya are gone, there are still more than 6 million Maya people living today. Their religion now is a mixture of Catholicism and their ancient beliefs.

Despite the pressures brought on by the modern world, some of the Maya have been able to hold on to their way of life in Central America and Mexico. Many Maya live in Guatemala, which is home to the ruins of the ancient city of Tikal. Many people of Maya **descent** still know how to speak a Mayan language.

Many Maya still work in agriculture, using the same techniques as their ancestors. They still pray at mountain temples using ancient rituals. Spiritual leaders still keep count on the sacred calendar and offer healing services and blessings. In their daily life, the Maya continue to keep their culture alive in the modern world.

GLOSSARY

archaeologist (ahr-kee-AH-luh-jihst): Someone who studies the tools and other objects left behind by ancient people.

cyclical (SIH-klih-kuhl): Happening again and again in the same order.

descent (dih-SENT): The background of a person in terms of their family or nationality.

drought (DROWT): A period of time during which there is very little or no rain.

equinox (EE-kwih-nahx): A day when day and night are the same length. This happens twice a year.

indigenous (ihn-DIH-juh-nuhs): Living naturally in a particular region.

pantheon (PAN-thee-ahn): The gods of a particular group of people.

patron (PAY-truhn): A god that protects a certain place or thing.

sacrificial (saa-kruh-FIH-shul): Having to do with someone or something being offered to a god or ruler.

sarcophagus (sahr-KAH-fuh-guhs): A stone coffin from ancient times.

scribe (SCRYB): A person from the past who was responsible for writing things down.

technique (tehk-NEEK): A particular skill or ability that someone uses to perform a job.

INDEX

PRIMARY SOURCE LIST

Page 8: Temple of the Inscriptions. Built by the Maya people around AD 675. Stone. Located at the ancient site of Palenque in Chiapas, Mexico.

Page 11: North Acropolis of Tikal. Built by the Maya people between 200 BC and AD 200. Stone. Located at the ancient site of Tikal in Petén Department, Guatemala.

Page 14: Carved stone head of Kukulkan on El Castillo pyramid. Built by the Maya people around AD 1000. Located at the ancient site of Chichén Itzá in Yucatán, Mexico.

Page 17: Sarcophagus lid of King Pakal from the Temple of Inscriptions. Built by the Maya people around AD 683. Now kept at the Temple of Inscriptions, Palenque, Mexico.

WEBSITES

Due to the changing nature of Internet links, PowerKids Press has developed an online list of websites related to the subject of this book. This site is updated regularly. Please use this link to access the list: www.powerkidslinks.com/soac/mayac